A MATTER OF
FAITH

Understanding True Religion

A MATTER OF
FAITH

Understanding True Religion

MART DE HAAN

DISCOVERY HOUSE
PUBLISHERS®

Feeding the Soul with the Word of God

P.O. Box 3566, Grand Rapids MI 49501-3566

Requests for permission to quote from this book
should be directed to:
Permissions Department
Discovery House Publishers
P.O. Box 3566
Grand Rapids, MI 49501

Cover design by Stan Myers
Cover photo by Karan Kapoor, Getty Images
Interior design by Steve Gier

ISBN: 978-1-57293-386-6

Printed in the United States of America

10 11 12 13 / DPI_RBC / 7 6 5 4 3 2 1

CONTENTS

INTRODUCTION

WHAT IS THE DIFFERENCE between religion and Christ?

A recent opinion poll found that 85 percent of Americans consider themselves somewhat or very religious. Whether such results indicate healthy spirituality is one of the questions that motivated the writing of this book.

Those of us who take comfort in our religious commitment might find ourselves unnerved by the fact that in Jesus' day He was feared and held in contempt by some of the most conservative and liberal religious leaders of his community.

This book is written with the conviction

that there can be great personal value in reflecting on the eternal difference between religious activity and a personal relationship with Christ. While the two can overlap and are often seen as synonymous, they are not the same. Practicing the former does not guarantee faith in the latter.

Together we'll see that prayers, charitable giving, and even personal sacrifice motivated by a desire to help others and win God's favor are no substitutes for reliance on the undeserved kindness of the One who lived and died in our place.

This book is also meant to help us see why "what we believe" even more than "what we do" needs a sense of careful self-examination. To consider that difference we'll review what we know about the Pharisees of Christ's day. Two thousand years later, they still give us a provocative example of a religious community that provides a striking contrast between what they and Jesus offered followers.

Religion or Christ? Which of these two choices is more important to knowing God and entering into a forever relationship with Him? Religion or Christ? What's the difference? It is a matter of faith. As we shall see, it can also be an eternal matter of life and death.

—MARTIN R. DE HAAN

RELIGION: DANGERS and DISTINCTIONS

The Dangers

FROM THE BEGINNING, religion has been dangerous.

Long before a Japanese nerve-gas cult terrorized unsuspecting Tokyo subway riders, people of faith have been killing one another in the name of God. Long before Waco and Jonestown betrayed the trust of members, spiritual fervor has taken the lives of those who were trying to gain the favor or God. Long before a group called Heaven's Gate led its members to take their own lives to meet their spiritual Source, splinter religious groups have brought immeasurable suffering on themselves and those they saw as "forces of darkness."

The danger of being religious can be seen as early as our first parents. Adam and Eve's fatal mistake occurred in an attempt to be more like God. Their error was not that they stopped believing in God, but that they began believing they could do something to increase their spirituality even though it meant doing the one thing God had told them not to do. Their ill-conceived effort to be like God on their terms rather than His became the seed of all false religions that eventually followed.

Unfortunately, Adam and Eve's "religious" mistakes resurfaced in their first son, Cain, who also tried to trust God on his own terms. Being a "tiller of the ground" rather than a "keeper of flocks" like his younger brother, Abel, Cain tried to worship God by offering a sacrifice from the "fruit of the ground." When God rejected Cain's act of worship and accepted Abel's, Cain became angry. Determined to have his "religion" his way, Cain rejected the counsel of God, killed his younger brother, and ruined his own life in the process.

Later in the unfolding story God's people, the nation of Israel repeatedly tried to serve and worship God in ways that were right in their own eyes. Even after all they had learned through the Exodus and forty years of learning to depend on God in the Wilderness, a number of Jewish men accepted an invitation to a pagan feast on the very threshold of the Promised Land. Under the influence of an idolatrous celebration, they entered into the worship of Baal and ate "sacrifices made to the dead" (Psalm 106:28). As a result, thousands of Jewish people died to show the danger of religion that is embraced in exchange for faith in the one true God (Numbers 25).

Saul, the first king of Israel made a similar mistake. He lost his kingdom by doing "religion" on his own terms. For instance, after assembling his army at Gilgal in preparation for a battle with the Philistines, he recalled that Samuel had told him to wait seven days until the prophet arrived to conduct pre-battle sacrifices for the army. But when Samuel was delayed in arriving, Saul decided he had no choice but to offer the sacrifice himself. So he told his men, " 'Bring a burnt offering and peace offerings here to me.' And [Saul] offered the burnt offering" (1 Samuel 13:9).

When Samuel finally arrived soon after Saul had made his offering, he told the king of Israel: "You have done foolishly. You have not kept the commandment of the Lord your God, which He commanded you" (1 Samuel 13:8-14; see also chapter 15). Saul must have thought that his actions were "spiritually minded" and therefore valuable. But he discovered that doing something "religious" instead of trusting God from the heart was a serious mistake.

As a result, Samuel told Saul: "Now your kingdom shall not continue" (13:14).

Even David got in trouble for trying to please God in his own way rather than making sure that he was listening to and trusting what God had said to Israel.

After being confirmed as king of Israel, he called for the sacred chest that contained the Ten Commandments of God. Then he proclaimed to all the assembly of Israel, "Let us bring the ark of our God back to us, for we have not inquired at it since the days of Saul" (1 Chronicles 13:3).

With enthusiasm, David led all Israel in a joyous procession to bring the holy object to Jerusalem. Yet when the oxen bearing the ark of the covenant stumbled, and when a priest named Uzza put out his hand to make sure that the ark did not fall, God struck the priest dead (13:9-10).

David reacted with fear and anger. How could he live with such a God? David had conducted a religious exercise—how could God not approve? How could God intervene so drastically in his efforts? Only after rereading the Law of God did David discover instructions for moving the "ark of God" that he and his people had ignored (1 Chronicles 13; 15:12-15).

Why does God make an issue of what we believe and how we serve and worship Him? He does so because He is looking for people who will worship Him in both spirit and truth (John 4:23-24)—not with an ever expanding or shrinking body of tradition. God wants to be worshiped from a heart that responds to the truth about His love and grace.

This may sound complex, but it isn't. All God really wants is for us to know and love His Son. He wants faith in Christ. And then, according to the New Testament, good religion will follow (James 1:26-27).

The Distinctions

Religion and faith in Christ are not mutually exclusive, but they are very distinct.

James, a New Testament writer and brother of Christ, wrote, "Pure and undefiled religion before God and the Father is this: to visit orphans and widows in their trouble, and to keep oneself unspotted from the world" (James 1:27). Notice that in this verse the concept of *religion* sounds very different from the ritual, liturgy, or traditions that we usually associate with the word. James reminds us that for religion to be good, it must express a heartfelt love for God and others.

Think about the difference between the actions James called for and the actions we usually associate with religion. True religion is an expression of faith—not a substitute for real trust and love.

No matter how closely religion and Christ are associated, the following comparison might help us to see how personal and infinite and eternal the differences are that we are considering.

Religion Is Something To Believe And Do:

- Attending religious services
- Enrolling children in religious schools
- Showing acts of kindness
- Avoiding immorality
- Believing in God
- Having religious affiliation
- Being baptized
- Receiving communion
- Studying doctrine
- Reading the Scriptures

- Offering prayers
- Celebrating religious events
- Teaching religious classes
- Giving aid to the poor
- Singing in the choir
- Being recognized as a godly person

Christ Is Someone To Know And Trust:

- Someone who is very near
- Someone who has authority to help us
- Someone who can forgive us
- Someone who can declare us righteous
- Someone who can set us apart for God
- Someone who can bring God to us
- Someone who can bring us to God
- Someone who can include us in His will
- Someone who can guide and teach us
- Someone who can be our example
- Someone who never leaves us all alone
- Someone who can be trusted
- Someone who can defend us

- Someone who can intercede for us
- Someone who can enable us
- Someone who can respond to our emotions
- Someone who can feel our pain
- Someone who can give us joy
- Someone who can give us peace
- Someone who can give us hope
- Someone who can give us love
- Someone who has proven His love for us
- Someone who has died for us
- Someone who rose from the dead for us
- Someone who can live His life through us
- Someone who can take us all the way Home
- Someone who can assure us of heaven

Religion or Christ? Two very different lists.
One is filled with activity that has something
to do with Jesus and what He has taught us in
the Bible. The other is filled with descriptions of
a person—a unique person who came to earth
to provide a plan of redemption for mankind.

Religion itself cannot provide that redemption. Only Christ can do that. That's why our faith is in Jesus, not religion.

■ APPLYING IT

- In the history of the people of the Old Testament, we see many examples of how they trusted religion rather than God. Can we see ourselves doing something similar today? How do we do that?
- What is the difference between worshiping God in spirit and in truth and worshiping Him in ritualism and ignorance? Do you know of any present-day examples?
- Looking at the list of religious activities, do you see anything wrong with them? What is the one thing those activities lack?

21

RELIGION
in JESUS' DAY

What Was It Like?

JESUS KNEW FIRSTHAND the dangers of religion. He was hated by some of the most religious people in Jerusalem. While the sinners and outcasts of society were attracted to Him, the religionists of His day—the Pharisees, scribes, Sadducees, and priests—were with few exceptions His bitter enemies.

Jesus didn't flatter these religious leaders. He didn't leave room for the notion that they were godly men who had just made a mistake about Him.

- In John 8 we read that He told the religious Pharisees that if they had known His Father, they would have known Him. When they asked Him, "Where is your father?" He responded with "You know neither Me nor My Father. If you had known Me, you would have known My Father also" (v. 19). Without realizing it, they had been so blinded by their own religious traditions and practices that they couldn't recognize the miracles, teaching, and goodness of their own long-awaited Messiah.

- In Matthew 23, we can sense Jesus' disappointment with these men of religion—the Pharisees. "Woe to you, scribes and Pharisees, hypocrites! For you shut up the kingdom of heaven against men" (v. 13). They worked diligently at their religious practices—yet Jesus did not see what they were doing as reflecting well on God. In fact, it appeared that they were working against the mercy and justice that Christ had come to show.

• In Matthew 15, we read that after the disciples asked Jesus a question about the Pharisees, He responded by saying they were "blind leaders

■ RELIGIOUS PEOPLE IN JESUS' DAY

PHARISEES—A Jewish religious group that attempted to keep Israel free of Gentile contamination by vigorously adhering to the Scriptures and to a large body of oral tradition that applied the Law of God to the details of daily life.

SCRIBES—Experts in biblical law (also called lawyers) who were often found among the Pharisees. The Pharisees depended on the scribes for a right interpretation of Scripture.

SADDUCEES—An upper-class Jewish religious group that rejected the oral tradition of the Pharisees and insisted on a rigid interpretation and adherence to the Mosaic Law.

PRIESTS—Descendants of Aaron who inherited the responsibility of attending to the ritual of the Temple in Jerusalem. They were often associated with the Sadducees.

of the blind" (v. 14). Clearly, their religion was not leading people in the right direction.

Knowing what we know about religious people today, this isn't the storyline many of us might expect, is it? We wouldn't expect Jesus' enemies to be the religious crowd.

Instead, we might expect Jesus' enemies to surface among the atheists, the secular thinkers, and the criminal elements of society. But that wasn't the case. Street people were attracted to Jesus. People with bad reputations were among His friends. Even Pilate, the pagan Roman governor of Judea, was inclined to give Jesus more consideration and benefit of the doubt. The religious Sadducees and Pharisees of Jerusalem, however, were always trying to discredit Jesus. They had no use for Him, and they were convinced that the world would be a better place without Him.

A Closer Look At The Pharisees. A lot of positive things could be said about the religious leaders that had issues with Jesus. Respected as some of the godliest and most spiritually committed of the Jews, they were

- **Theists** who because of their belief in the God of Israel advocated a God-centered life.
- **Separatists** who were determined to protect Israel from being compromised, swallowed, and absorbed into a Gentile world.
- **Biblicists** who believed that Israel's future depended on whether or not they honored and practiced the Law of God.
- **Populists,** many of whom were craftsmen and tradesmen, therefore identifying with the common man.
- **Pragmatists** who wrestled not only with what the Law said but also with how it looked and applied to the smallest details of life.
- **Traditionalists** who carefully memorized, repeated, and entrenched themselves in the ways of their spiritual forefathers.

The Pharisees, however, took some wrong turns in their attempt to come to terms with the moral laws of God. As they made an effort to show what the Word of God "looked like" in daily life, their concrete applications became not only an end in themselves but even a way of avoiding the spirit and intent of Moses. Before long, they were lost in specifics, and according to Jesus they were "teaching as doctrines the commandments of men" (Matthew 15:9). They focused on the details and lost the heart.

Why Was Christ a Threat?

Religionists saw Jesus as dangerous. He caused a commotion that threatened to destabilize the delicate religious and political balance of power in Israel.

He had a reputation for doing unexplainable things. He taught with an air of authority, and He shifted attention from external matters of religion to internal attitudes of the heart. He taught that God is not looking for people who are doing well in their religion. Instead, he told them He was looking for

- **The poor in spirit**, who recognize their dependence on God in every area of life.
- **Those who mourn**, grieving the nature and results of sin in themselves or in others.
- **The meek**, who are willing to live under the authority of God.
- **Those who hunger and thirst for righteousness**, accepting the rightness that comes from God.
- **Those who are merciful**, giving undeserved relief to others in the face of misery.
- **The pure in heart**, who are clean on the inside.
- **The peacemakers**, who are working to

reconcile people to their God and to each other (Matthew 5:1-9).

Together, these foundational principles and attitudes of Jesus' Sermon on the Mount showed why He was regarded as a threat to the religious crowd and loved by the most unlikely of people.

30

Christ resisted the proud while showing kindness to broken people. While the Pharisees took pride in their knowledge of moral and spiritual Law, Jesus showed mercy to those condemned by the religious. As a result, Jewish spiritual leaders feared that Jesus was showing disregard for the laws of Moses. What they didn't realize was that no one would fulfill the spirit of the 600-plus laws of Moses more than those who knew that they were loved, forgiven, and fully accepted by God.

Years later, an apostle of Christ and former

Pharisee named Paul argued that religious laws never had never saved anyone from sin and never could save anyone from sin—nor could they produce the kind of heartfelt attitudes that give honor to God. In several New Testament letters, Paul reasoned that the Law was given to show our need of a Savior who was superior to religion in every way possible.

One often-quoted example of Paul's confidence in faith rather than in religion can be found in his letter to the Romans, in which he said,

> *Therefore by the deeds of the law no flesh will be justified in His sight, for by the law is the knowledge of sin. But now the righteousness of God apart from the law is revealed, being witnessed by the Law and the Prophets, even the righteousness of God, through faith in Jesus Christ (Romans 3:20-22).*

Christ is superior to religion in any direction you look:

• **Look Back**—He is the Creator and eternal Word who was not only with God from the beginning but who also was actually God himself. "In the beginning was the Word, and the Word was with God, and the Word was God. He [Jesus] was in the beginning with God. All things were made through Him, and without Him nothing was made that was made" (John 1:1-3).

• **Look Ahead**—He is our coming King and Judge who will one day rule the earth and judge every heart. "This same Jesus, who was taken up from you into heaven, will so come in like manner as you saw Him go into heaven (Acts 1:11). "For it is written, 'As I live, says the Lord, every knee shall bow to Me, and every tongue shall confess to God' " (Romans 14:11).

• **Look Up**—He is our Savior and Lord who alone can reach down and save us while at the same time provide a lordship that's loving and wise (John 3:13-16; Philippians 2:9-11).

• **Look Down**—He holds us in His own hands as our Provider and Sustainer. "For by [Jesus] all things were created that are in heaven and that are on earth, visible and invisible, whether thrones or dominions or principalities or powers" (Colossians 1:16).

• **Look Right**—As we turn to the "right" to see what God affirms, He becomes our Teacher and Example. "He who says he abides in Him ought himself also to walk just as He walked" (1 John 2:6; see also 1 Peter 2:21).

• **Look Left**—As we turn away from what is "right," and therefore to what is wrong, He becomes our Intercessor and Advocate. "If anyone sins, we have an Advocate with the Father, Jesus Christ the righteous (1 John 2:1; see also verse 2).

• **Look Within**—He is our Life, our Peace, and our Strength (Galatians 2:20; Colossians 1:27).

This is the all-encompassing Person the Pharisees missed. How did they miss Him? How could they wait eagerly with all Israel for the coming Messiah, only to want to kill Him when He came? Let's take a closer look at what Jesus himself said.

What Mistakes Did the Pharisees Make?

In Luke 11, Jesus confronted the Pharisees with several deficiencies of their religion. Let's see what their faults tell us not only about the Pharisees but also about ourselves.

The Pharisees settled for looking good

A few years ago, a major chemical company ran a series of image-changing advertisements designed to convince the public that it was concerned about the environment. The television evening news carried the story of a group of protesters who weren't convinced that the company was as concerned as it claimed to be.

34

One protester held up a sign that named the company. It read: "We won't be fooled. Clean up your act, not just your image."

The protester's sign reminds me of what Jesus said to the Pharisees. In Luke 11:39, He likens them to group of dishwashers who clean the outside of a container while leaving the inside dirty. He said:

> *You Pharisees make the outside of the cup and dish clean, but your inward part is full of greed and wickedness. Foolish ones! Did not He who made the outside make the inside also? But rather give alms of such things as you have; then indeed all things are clean to you (vv.39-41).*

Jesus was referring to the careful and technically exact ritual of hand washing that Pharisees practiced before sitting down to meal. They washed before eating and between courses—not for cleanliness reasons but because they prided themselves in fulfilling their ceremonial law. Jesus knew, however, that the "ritually clean" religion of the Pharisees didn't go below the surface. Their image was good, but their act was bad.

Religion never changes the heart of the problem. It deals with surface issues. That's why on another occasion Jesus told a Pharisee and ruler of the Jews that he needed to be born again (an internal, spiritual birth) if he was ever going to see and be a part of God's kingdom (John 3). The man's name was Nicodemus, and he was part of the Jewish ruling council. He would have known his religion inside and out. But he had seen something in Jesus that his ritual was not touching, so he visited Jesus at night to ask Him some questions. Surely the answers surprised him—for Jesus said nothing about religion, rituals, rites, or rules. Instead he talked about spiritual rebirth—a new and mysterious concept to Nicodemus.

We can be like Nicodemus. We can

accumulate religious activities only to discover that prayers, communions, confirmations, baptisms, or volunteering for church causes—while looking good and feeling good—lack spiritual, life-changing power. The truth is, standing on form won't fool God. Jesus told Nicodemus, "That which is born of the flesh is flesh, and that which is born of the Spirit is spirit" (John 3:6). Putting our faith in Christ can do for an individual what all of the religion in the world could never do (John 3:16).

The story of the salvation of George Whitfield, a British preacher who was instrumental in spreading the Great Awakening revival of the eighteenth century into America, points out the value of Christ over religion. When he was sixteen, he became convicted of his sin. So he began to do all the religious things he knew how—including fasting for thirty-six hours. During the Lenten season, he says, "[I] almost starved myself to death." Still, he was miserable spiritually. Finally, he met Charles Wesley, who pointed him toward John 3 and the idea of being born again. He put his faith in Jesus and became one of the most influential preachers of the 1700s. And more often than not, he spoke on the passage, "You must be born again."

Doing religion may make a person feel better temporarily, but trusting Christ does something far more important. It changes the heart. It brings the Source of love within us. It's a humbling process. It means acknowledging the worthlessness of our external clean-ups, giving ourselves over to the mercy of God and trusting Him to do through the Spirit of Christ what we could never do for ourselves. It is recognizing that a clean heart—not clean hands—is what we really need.

The Pharisees made much of little

I envy people who are good at the game *Trivial*

Pursuit. They have a mind and memory for detail that must give them a great advantage in life over people like me. I sometimes can't remember the name of a friend or where I put my glasses.

Like all other strengths, however, a capacity for trivia can become a weakness if not kept in check. Jesus described the dangers of getting lost in details when He told the Pharisees that one fault of their religion was to major on minor issues.

> *Woe to you Pharisees! For you tithe mint and rue and all manner of herbs, and pass by justice and the love of God. These you ought to have done, without leaving the others undone (Luke 11:42).*

In other words, the little things have their place as long as we don't let them get in the way of the more important issues. The Pharisees were not wrong in their tithing, but they were wrong in neglecting the more important matters of showing justice to others and love to God. Bible scholar Darrell Bock puts it like this: "Jesus condemns the Pharisees' selectivity in choosing to follow only certain minor rules while consistently ignoring the important matters" (*Baker Exegetical Commentary on the New Testament*, p. 1116).

The Pharisees were the logicians of Judaism. They made a science of carrying the Law to its logical conclusions. They prided themselves in their ability to think a matter through down to the smallest detail. When they tithed, for instance, they gave a percentage of all their increase. If they owed God a tenth of the harvest, they would give God 10 percent of everything, including their herbs, even though the Law specifically said that it wasn't necessary to do so.

The Pharisees' willingness to do more than what was required was not bad. Their mistake was that in attending to these numerous details they forgot to love. According to Jesus, that means they ended up missing the whole point of the Law (Matthew 22:37-40). When the Pharisees asked Jesus what the key to the Law was, He surprised them by telling them that it was two things they had not thought of putting first: Loving God with their whole heart and loving others as much as they loved themselves. "On these two commandments hang all the Law and the Prophets," Jesus told them (v.40).

The Pharisees were like the man who goes to the auto dealer to buy a new car. While there, he notices some accessories that seem to be just what he needs to add a touch of class to his new "wheels." An hour later he leaves the showroom with a smile, clutching his purchase of a coffee mug, a dash compass, a map holder, and the manufacturer's keychain. Like the Pharisees, he leaves with more than he came with—and less. With trinkets in hand, he gets in his old car and heads for home.

Religion, as good and necessary as it is, can fill us up with lesser details that easily get the better part of our attention. What makes this problem difficult to detect is that the process of getting good at the fine points of Bible study, prayer, or giving can feel like it's working when it isn't. There's no substitute for a heart of love and justice that reflects a right relationship with God himself.

A few years after Christ ascended into heaven following His resurrection, the apostle Paul repeated Jesus' teaching to distracted Christians in Corinth. He made it clear that even spiritual gifts, knowledge, faith, and self-sacrifice are trivial pursuits if done without the love of God (1 Corinthians 13).

In that passage, Paul contrasted what seemed to be religious activities with the way those things appear to God if there is no love.

• If a believer speaks angelic messages without doing so with godly love, he might as well be mute.

• If a believer speaks mighty words of prophecy without doing so in godly love, he might as well be speaking gibberish.

• If a believer empties his pocketbook on the needy without doing so in godly love, he may as well have kept his coins.

• If a believer sacrifices his body without doing so in godly love, he may as well have stayed home that day.

43

The truth is hard to take for those who major in the minors and spend their time on peripheral religious activity. And that truth is this: Every pursuit is trivial if not done in the love of the God of salvation and because of faith in Christ.

The Pharisees loved the approval of others

Religion can be one of the biggest ego trips around. What deserves more honorable mention from others in our lives than to be recognized as a good and moral person? Or what plays more to our sense of self-importance and pride than to be thought of as someone of whom God approves?

It might seem better to be recognized as a good person than as unprincipled. Wouldn't it be better to be known as a priest or a pastor than as pornographer or prostitute? Maybe not. Jesus said that unless something changed, the Pharisees were going to the same hell as those who boldly rejected God. The only difference was that Jesus reserved His most severe criticism for religious people who were using their spiritual reputation to get social attention and honors. To the religionist Jesus said:

> *Woe to you Pharisees! For you love the best seats in the synagogues and greetings in the marketplaces (Luke 11:43).*

We all love to be appreciated by others.

44

We love to be approved by those who see
something praiseworthy in us. That's not bad.
What is bad, however, is when the opinions of
others become more important to us than the
opinions of God. What's dangerous is when
the flattery and approving attention of others
becomes like a narcotic, numbing us to our lack
of love for others, to the presence and mind of
God, and to the fact that in our sober moments
we know that our reputation is far better than
we are.

45

Being good at the rules of religion enables
us to bask in the praise of others. Submitting
to Christ, however, is the only way to have the
favor of God. This is true even after a person
has put his or her faith in Christ and entered
into the religious experience of the church. The
question of whether we are going to play to the
grandstands or to God continues to be an issue
for as long as we live.

Unfortunately, we have become all too

familiar with people who grew enamored with their own fame as Christian leaders. Playing by the rules of religion outwardly, they allowed the adoring crowds to guide their thinking. No longer led by the Spirit and by the gentle voice of the Savior, they played to the crowds or played their own game in private. And then, through either a lack of humility or a loss of morality, they came crashing down. Learning to be good at rules but forsaking Jesus and His love, they demonstrated the emptiness of religiosity devoid of Christlikeness.

The apostle Paul knew what it was like to struggle with human criticism and to be found unacceptable by members of one's own spiritual family. That's why he wrote to critics in Corinth:

> With me it is a very small thing that I should be judged by you or by human court. In fact, I do not even judge myself. For I

know of nothing against myself, yet I am not justified by this; but He who judges me is the Lord (1 Corinthians 4:3-4).

Later, Paul wrote:

We dare not class ourselves or compare ourselves with those who commend themselves. But they, measuring themselves by themselves, and comparing themselves among themselves, are not wise (2 Corinthians 10:12).

47

Paul had learned to take criticism with grace—not because it didn't hurt but because he had found that human recognition and honor don't count (Philippians 3:1-10). All that counts is hearing Christ say, "Well-done, good and faithful servant." Paul had been a Pharisee. He knew the difference between being recognized by religion and being approved by Christ.

The Pharisees practiced coverup rather than disclosure

"Hi, my name is Joe, and I'm an alcoholic." Recognizing the presence of the problem is like reaching first base in the Alcoholics Anonymous path of recovery. Unfortunately, it's an element of humility that is all too often missing in religion. One of the most common feelings among church-goers is the disconnected sense of being with people who aren't being real. They feel shoulder-to-shoulder but far apart from people who put on Sunday clothes and Sunday faces to go through the motions of Sunday worship.

Many like it that way. They don't mind the anonymity—the freedom of not having to open up to fellow worshipers. Others, however, are crying out on the inside. "Wait," they say. "This isn't right. This isn't real. We've all got problems. Why can't we admit our struggles with worry, anger, fear, envy, bitterness, shame, and lust so we can encourage and comfort and hold each other accountable?" They know that hiding behind a cloak of invincibility doesn't do them any good.

Jesus would agree. He said:

Woe to you, scribes and Pharisees, hypocrites! For you are like graves which are not seen, and the men who walk over them are not aware of them (Luke 11:44).

The following story from *The People's Almanac #2* illustrates a similar problem of dishonesty:

Once when Prussian King Frederick the Great visited Potsdam Prison, every convict he spoke to claimed to be innocent. Finally he came across one man under sentence of death for stealing who simply said, "Your Majesty, I am guilty and richly deserving of punishment." Frederick turned to the prison governor and said, "Free this rascal and get him out of our prison, before he corrupts all the noble innocent people in here."

From God's point of view, religious people can be like that prison community. Religious beliefs, ritual, and association often give people a way of denying their shame, guilt, and need of forgiveness. Instead of encouraging people to declare their in-ability to save themselves, religion can give people a front and cover for their unresolved problems.

Our effort to gloss over our problems with religious activity is a self-protective reaction that goes back to the beginning of human history. After our first parents sinned, they were stunned by their loss of innocence. They used fig leaves to cover themselves and fled among the trees to hide themselves from the presence of the Lord. When the Lord came into the Garden, Adam admitted that he had hidden himself because he was afraid.

People have been hiding themselves behind

50

the trees of religious activity and behind the fig leaves of human effort ever since. Rather than humbling ourselves and admitting our need of Christ's saving death and saving life, we try to do enough religion to compensate for our sins.

In the process of getting all tied up in religion, we hide ourselves from Christ, who offers His mercy only to those who humble themselves in needy and broken honesty.

The Pharisees added to life's burdens

Imagine what it would be like to have two kinds of people in the world: brick givers and brick takers. Every time you meet one of them, a brick is either added to your pile or one is taken off. Jesus would be one of the brick-takers. The Pharisees would be brickgivers. This function of religion became apparent as Jesus responded to a question posed by a lawyer of the Pharisees (an expert in biblical law on whom the Pharisees depended). Jesus said:

Woe to you also, lawyers! For you load men with burdens hard to bear, and you yourselves do not touch the burdens with one of your fingers (Luke 11:46).

Jesus knew His audience. These religious experts attached hundreds of additional obligations to the Law of God. Yet they themselves were masters of the loophole. They even had ways of sidestepping the law of the Sabbath, which forbade carrying a burden on that day.

Scottish theologian William Barclay quotes pharisaic tradition, which said:

He who carries anything, whether it be in his right hand, or in his left hand, or in his bosom, or on his shoulder is guilty; but he who carries anything on the back of his hand, or with his foot, or with his mouth, or with his elbow, or with his hair, or with his money-bag turned upside down, or between his moneybag and his shirt, or in the fold of his shirt, or in his shoe, or in his sandal is guiltless, because he does not carry it in the usual way of carrying it out.

Religious insiders still practice the art of brick giving—of adding to the burdens of others—while having ways of excusing themselves from the obligations they place on others. For instance, many religious leaders teach that daily family devotions is a must, while acknowledging that they themselves have reasons for not being able to do it. Also, many religious people teach that Christians under grace, while not being under the law of the tithe, should start with the legal requirement of 10-percent giving and then add to it. Other religious teachers insist that God hates and prohibits divorce under all circumstances. But they know that God Himself divorced Israel because of her prolonged spiritual adultery, and they know that

Moses the lawgiver permitted divorce because of the hardness of people's hearts (Deuteronomy 24:1-4; Matthew 19:1-9).

By contrast, Jesus consistently upheld the high ideals of the Law while making merciful provisions for the repentant sinner. Jesus understood the healthy tension between the holiness and the love of God when He said:

Come to Me, all you who labor and are heavy laden, and I will give you rest. Take My yoke upon you and learn from Me, for I am gentle and lowly in heart, and you will find rest for your souls. For My yoke is easy and My burden is light (Matthew 11:28-30).

The Pharisees deceived themselves

I've heard it jokingly said, "I love everybody. It's people I can't stand." The Pharisees acted out a similar phrase without trying to be funny. Jesus said that the Pharisees prided themselves in honoring and building memorials to the prophets. The irony is that when they met a real Prophet, they wanted to kill Him. Barclay says:

> The only prophets they admired were dead prophets; when they met a living one, they tried to kill Him. They honored the dead prophets with tombs and memorials, but they dishonored the living ones with persecution and death.

This is the point Jesus made in Luke 11:47-51 and in a parallel passage in Matthew 23 when He said:

> *Woe to you, scribes and Pharisees, hypocrites! Because you build the tombs of the prophets and adorn the monuments of the righteous, and say, "If we had lived in the days of our fathers, we wouldn't have been partakers with them in the*

blood of the prophets." Therefore you are witnesses against yourselves that you are sons of those who murdered the prophets. Fill up, then, the measure of your fathers' guilt (vv. 29-32).

The Pharisees had fooled themselves. They didn't think of themselves as prophet killers or Messiah killers. They didn't realize that their empty religion actually made them enemies of God. The flesh has always been at war with the Spirit. Religion is powerless to restrain the self-centered, self-protective obsessions of the flesh. It takes a living Christ to change the human heart.

A pattern of behavior repeats itself time after time when people give themselves to religion rather than to Christ—just as happened with the religious people Jesus confronted. For example, with their lips "religious people" may even think they are honoring God and the Scriptures, but when a child or a mate has the boldness to confess Christ as Savior they suddenly see red. They think the loved one has gone too far.

Very religious parents have been known to resent the fact that their child thinks there was something wrong with the religion in which he was born, baptized, and confirmed. Parents who have been churchgoers all of their lives are often incensed to hear a son or daughter talk about being "born again," the very words Jesus used when talking to a Pharisee named Nicodemus (John 3:1-16). Religious parents who resent the fact that their child wants to put their faith in Christ need to do some serious soul-searching. A negative reaction to a son or daughter who says that he or she has accepted Christ is a fairly strong indicator that the parent is in the same condition of self-deception as the scribes and Pharisees our Lord lovingly but firmly confronted.

The Pharisees took away the key of knowledge

One of the greatest dangers of religion is that it causes us to be a danger not only to ourselves but also to others. To the very religious biblical experts of His day Jesus said:

> "Woe to you lawyers! For you have taken away the key of knowledge. You did not enter in yourselves, and those who were entering in you hindered." And as He said these things to them, the scribes and the Pharisees began to assail Him vehemently, and to cross-examine Him about many things, lying in wait for Him, and seeking to catch Him in something He might say, that they might accuse Him (Luke 11:52-54).

Here Jesus said that religionists who were against Him had taken away from the people "the key of knowledge." What was the key Jesus had in mind? There seem to be a number of possibilities. The Pharisees, for instance, took away the key of knowledge from "the man on the street" (1) by replacing the Word of God with tradition and trivia, (2) by attempting to discredit Christ (John 14:6), and (3) by distracting others from a "right attention of heart" (the "window of light" in Luke 11:33-35).

While the Scriptures and Christ are both keys of knowledge, I believe that Jesus was probably referring to the key of "a right attention of heart." If the heart has the "right attention," it will be focused on the Scriptures and Christ. The section of Luke 11 we've been looking at is preceded by verses 33-35, where Jesus said:

No one, when he has lit a lamp, puts it in a secret place or under a basket, but on a lampstand, that those who come in may see the light. The lamp of the body is the eye. Therefore, when your eye is good, your

whole body also is full of light. But when
your eye is bad, your body also is full of
darkness. Therefore take heed that the light,
which is in you is not darkness.

In other words, if a person's "lamp" (his eye or attention of heart) is right, then he will be filled with the knowledge of God. But if his "lamp" is obstructed, then a person will be full of darkness (empty of the light and knowledge of God). Bible scholar Darrell Bock puts it like this: "Those who would hear Jesus are to be constantly on the watch that what they take in is light, not darkness" (*Baker Exegetical Commentary on the New Testament*, p. 1101).

As Jesus was teaching these truths about the lamp of the body and the key of knowledge, He was invited to a Pharisee's house for dinner. As it turned out, Jesus completed His lesson around the dinner table.

The Pharisee helped Jesus set up His teaching

by pointing out—with surprise—that Jesus had not washed before partaking of the meal. While this was not a commandment laid down in the law, ceremonial washing had been added to the list in the Pharisaical law code.

As a dinner guest of a Pharisee, Jesus pointed to the light-blocking obstacles that the Pharisees had placed over their own eyes (their attention of heart). The Teacher showed them that by their religious externalism ("you Pharisees clean the outside of the cup and dish" v.39 NIV), their majoring on minors, their love for approval ("you love the best seats in the synagogues" v.43 NIV), their selfish coverup, their legalistic brick-giving, and their self-deception that they had not only lost the light for themselves but also for others. In this way, they had taken away the key of knowledge.

The Pharisees made converts to hell

Imagine being given a key by a trusted religious

leader. You put the key in a door labeled "destiny," and when you open it you find yourself looking into the flames of hell. The Pharisees were setting up their converts for that kind of terrible surprise. In a passage very similar to Luke 11, Jesus said:

> *Woe to you, scribes and Pharisees, hypocrites! For you travel land and sea to win one proselyte, and when he is won, you make him twice as much a son of hell as yourselves (Matthew. 23:15).*

Jesus may have called the religious converts "twice as much a son of hell" because converts are often more zealous for their faith than those who have come to take their faith for granted. Proselytes have made a major change of life and are ready to defend and promote it with fresh enthusiasm. They know they don't have all the answers, but they trust their leaders, who supposedly know much more than they do.

This kind of trust would put the Pharisees' converts in real jeopardy. Since Jesus called the Pharisees "blind leaders of the blind" (Matthew 15:14), their followers would be doubly bound. Not only is the new convert still spiritually blind but he also has unknowingly placed himself in the trust of a religious teacher who cannot see where either of them is going.

The problem with religion is that in matters of ultimate and most extreme importance it offers hope where there is no hope. For that reason, an atheist or agnostic is probably in a safer place than the person who has been converted to religion. At least the atheist or agnostic is not apt to assume mistakenly that he has made peace with God. The atheist or agnostic is not expecting any rewards or punishment—just annihilation. The religious person, however, can wrongly think he knows what he has to do to make it to heaven, or to walk with God—even if he is not sure that he's "quite there" yet.

The implications are stunningly severe. Religionists such as the Pharisees and their converts are headed for a terrible awakening—a jolting surprise with eternal consequences. Jesus assured us of this when He said:

> *I say to you, that unless your righteousness exceeds the righteousness of the Scribes and Pharisees, you will by no means enter the kingdom of heaven (Matthew 5:20).*

Put yourself in the place of a misguided religious convert. You think you have chosen to be a good person. You recognize the error of those who have no place in their heart for God. You feel pity for people who show by their behavior and associations that they are willing to risk eternity for a few more hours of forbidden pleasure. You think you've chosen better. You've found a pastor, a priest, or a rabbi that you like. You trust him, and you are confident that he is good man who would never be an enemy of God. You like it when he leads you in religious ceremony that helps you to feel closer to God and better about yourself.

However, that leader, while helping you master the religious elements of life and even urging you to perform the rituals of the church, never introduces you to Christ. Oh, you may have heard of Jesus, and you may have even heard His name mentioned, but you are never introduced to Him personally. You do religion, but you never put your faith in Jesus. The key you have is clearly marked "religion," and you trust it.

The true test of your activity comes when it is too late to change. Once you put the key he gives you into the lock on the door marked "destiny," you discover to your horror that it's too late. You discover that the door opens to an everlasting life of separation from God. You discover that you had the wrong key.

The reality is that *faith in religion* leads to the dead end of unfulfilled eternal expectations. *Faith in Christ,* however, leads to an open door into an eternal life enjoying the glories of heaven and the comfort of God's presence.

■ APPLYING IT

- In what sense are true followers of Jesus treated with distrust by religious leaders today?

- Do you see yourself in any of the descriptions under "A Closer Look At The Pharisees"?

- How can we sometimes settle for "looking good" as the Pharisees did instead of being concerned about what God truly wants from us?

- What could be some trivial pursuits that

we chase down without God's love to guide us?

- What are some ways to ensure that we don't dwell on the approval of others instead of the approval of God?
- How could we possibly take away the key of knowledge from others by our actions—even our religiosity?
- Who do you know who has *faith in religion* and needs to be gently directed toward *faith in Christ* instead?

LESSONS from a CONVERTED RELIGIONIST

Learning From Paul

THERE WERE ABOUT six thousand Pharisees living in Israel at the time of Christ. As we have noted, they had a reputation for holding lengthy discussions on such "fine points" as whether it was lawful to eat an egg that had been laid on the Sabbath. In actuality, this issue came down to whether the hen was a laying hen or one being fattened for consumption. A Sabbath egg that came from the former was off limits; one that was produced by the latter was acceptable. Such were the discussions of the religionists known as Pharisees.

Saul of Tarsus (later known as the apostle Paul) inherited this religious tradition. He described himself as "a Pharisee and the son of a Pharisee" (Acts 23:6). Before his life-changing encounter with Christ as recorded in Acts 9, Saul believed that his standing with God was determined by his relationship to the Law—by his religious experience. In fact, he explained his "pre-Christ" days by saying, "I was thoroughly trained in the law of our fathers and was just as zealous for God as any of you are today" (Acts 22:3 NIV).

After his conversion, though, Paul defined his standing with God in new terms. Now what counted was his relationship to Christ. In Romans 3:21-22, Paul wrote, "But now the righteousness of God apart from the law is revealed, . . . even the righteousness of God, through faith in Jesus Christ to all and on all who believe."

Paul became concerned about faith in Christ—showing the love of Christ to others and reminding fellow believers that everyone will one day answer personally to Christ the Lord.

When it came to arguable issues of scriptural application, Paul was no longer pre-occupied with the legal rulings of the scribes. Instead he pled with other members of the family in questionable matters. In his letter to the Romans he wrote:

71

> *Who are you to judge another's servant? . . .*
> *So then each of us shall give account of*
> *himself to God. Therefore let us not judge*
> *one another anymore, but rather resolve this,*
> *not to put a stumbling block or a cause to fall*
> *in our brother's way (14:4,12-13).*

Many of us need to learn from Paul's "after Christ" point of view. In an attempt to protect ourselves from compromise, we adopt his "pre-Christ" perspective. Adopting the way of the Pharisees, we develop our own lists of what a follower of Christ will or will not do. The only trouble is that someone could keep every point on some of our lists and still be no closer to God. A person could "religiously" refrain from alcohol, immorality, tobacco, and gambling, and still be godless. A person could attend church, give money, offer prayers, and read the Bible while still being angry, critical, and mean.

72

What counts, however, is what comes from the Holy Spirit, not what comes from the flesh. Christlike attitudes of love, which are so different from our natural inclinations, drive us to the Spirit of Christ for wisdom, enablement, and a fresh assurance of forgiveness. It is better to let our struggle with unkeepable principles drive us to faith in Christ than it is to occupy ourselves with the formalities of religion and miss Jesus altogether.

■ APPLYING IT

- Sure, we can think the Pharisees were silly to discuss egg-laying and the Sabbath, but they are not alone. What are some "church" discussions you've heard about that have divided people into separate camps?

- What does Paul's phrase, "the righteousness apart from the law" mean? How does it relate to true salvation?

- Have you ever thought that you have a "pre-Christ" perspective? How is that possible for a truly born again child of God?

RELIGION
or CHRIST:
FINAL
CONSIDERATIONS

Dangers of Application

MANY OF US BELIEVE that Bible study must be accompanied by questions like, "What difference does it make?" and "How does it apply to my life?" We have seen how prior generations could preoccupy themselves with a study of Revelation, Daniel, and the Minor Prophets without coming to terms with the problems in their lives that made them anxious, hierarchical, competitive, unemotional, demanding, critical, mean, and possessive. We feel that to avoid that mistake, we must seek application in our study.

Certainly, it is good to struggle with questions like "What will this truth look like in my life?" But that is also how prior generations came up with their lists of what Christian living "looks like." They don't smoke (unless they're burning with anger), they don't drink (unless they're getting wired with coffee), they don't enjoy questionable entertainment (unless it involves gossip).

This was the kind of thing the Pharisees were so good at as well.

So we have to rethink how this works. We have to realize that when rules of application become our principles and when actions replace attitudes of the heart, we have probably given in to a religion that has replaced Christ rather than one that serves Him. Our actions and our decisions about how to live need to flow from our love for and our faith in Christ and our appreciation for what He has done for us rather than from our attempts to use application to get close to God.

Refraining from or engaging in certain activities as a test of godliness leads to empty religiosity. Doing the same out of our serious love for Christ and our desire to serve and honor Him is not about religion but about our relationship and fellowship with Him. Again, it's a matter of religion or true faith in Jesus Christ.

Why Focus on Christ?

In exchange for our trust in Him, Christ does many things for us that religion cannot do. We can examine this list as a reminder that religion cannot reward us as Jesus does. Keeping rituals and honoring traditions of a religion do not lead to the comfort, care, love, and concern that comes our way when we put our faith in the person of Jesus

Christ. Notice what our Savior Jesus does for us.

- He loves us (John 15:13; Romans 8:35).
- He brings us to God (1 Timothy 2:5).
- He brings God to us (Colossians 1:15).
- He bought us for God (Ephesians 1:7).
- He defends us before God (1 John 2:1).
- He declares us "not guilty" (Romans 3:24; 5:1).
- He reconciles us to God (2 Corinthians 5:19).
- He sets us apart for God (1 Corinthians 1:30).
- He gives us peace with God (Romans 5:1).
- He makes us acceptable to God (Ephesians 1:6).
- He forgives us (Ephesians 1:7).
- He frees us from bondage (Romans 8:2).
- He qualifies us for adoption (Ephesians 1:5).
- He makes us heirs of God (Ephesians 1:11).
- He gives us His Spirit (John 14:16-17).
- He gives us a new focus (Colossians 3:1-2).
- He lives within us (Colossians 1:27).
- He brings us into God's family (John 1:12).
- He intercedes for us (Romans 8:34).

- He rescues us from Satan's power
  (Colossians 1:13).
- He places us into God's kingdom
  (Colossians 1:13).
- He gives us eternal life (Romans 6:23).
- He shows us how to live (1 John 2:6).

A Study In Contrasts

There are two sides to many issues in Scripture. This is true of the subject of religion. To keep a balanced view, it's important for us to live with the tension of two seemingly contradictory ideas.

Religion Is Important
The Bible tells us of many religious practices that either (1) point us to God or (2) provide a channel for expressing our relationship to God. Both Old and New Testaments contain religious

law, principle, belief, and ritual. If we think of religion as action or conduct indicating belief in, reverence for, and a desire to please God through our faith in Jesus Christ, then it is clear that this kind of religion provides

- a pattern of doctrine and belief (Titus 2:1).
- a shared experience (Acts 2:37-47; Hebrews 10:25).
- an outward show of inner faith (1 John 3:17-18).

80

Religion Is Worthless

Religion is worthless if we depend on any external actions to make us right with God. Whether before salvation or after, no amount of religious knowledge or action can save us. Knowledge or action can only give us a way of expressing our personal faith in Christ. In that sense we must avoid religious activity that gives us

- attempts to earn salvation (Ephesians 2:8-10).

- any thought of perfecting ourselves (Galatians 3:1-3).
- anything that displaces Christ (Colossians 2:6-8).

Religion is dangerous, not because it is bad but because it is often good enough to turn our trust away from Christ. Our tendency is to reject confidence in what Christ can do and replace it with something that we can do for ourselves.

81

Defining Our Terms

To help understand completely what we have been trying to explain in this book, it might help to review some vital terms that relate to the question of whether religion or faith is what we need when we stand before God. Understanding these terms in their proper context can help to clarify what the Bible says about this all-important subject.

Christ—the second person of the triune God. Jesus became a member of the human race, lived a sinless life, was crucified, and rose from the dead to offer salvation to all who put their faith in Him.

Words to think about: "Jesus said to him, 'I am the way, the truth, and the life. No one comes to the Father except through Me' " (John 14:6).

Communion—symbolic ceremony of bread and wine to remind believers of Christ's death for them.

Words to think about: "The Lord Jesus on the same night in which He was betrayed took bread; and when He had given thanks, He broke it and said, 'Take, eat; this is My body which is broken for you; do this in remembrance of Me.' In the same manner He also took the cup after supper, saying, 'This cup is the new covenant in My blood. This do, as

often as you drink it, in remembrance of Me' "
(1 Corinthians 11:23-25).

Cross—the form of execution by which Christ
suffered and died in our place to pay the penalty
for our sins.

Words to think about: "For the message
of the cross is foolishness to those who are
perishing, but to us who are being saved it is
the power of God" (1 Corinthians 1:18).

Faith—personal trust which, when placed in
the person of Christ, forms the heart of true
religion.

Words to think about: "For by grace you
have been saved through faith, and that not of
yourselves; it is the gift of God, not of works, lest
anyone should boast" (Ephesians 2:8-9).

Justification—to be declared righteous. In
salvation, God extends to all who trust in

Christ the legal status of being right with Him.

Words to think about: "But you were washed, but you were sanctified, but you were justified in the name of the Lord Jesus and by the Spirit of our God" (1 Corinthians 6:11).

Legalist—someone who trusts the Law or man-made rules to do for him what only Christ can do.

Words to think about: "The Pharisee stood and prayed thus with himself, 'God, I thank You that I am not like other men—extortioners, unjust, adulterers, or even as this tax collector. I fast twice a week; I give tithes of all that I possess.' " Jesus said of this man, "Everyone who exalts himself will be humbled" (Luke 18:11,14).

Religion—a system of thought and conduct expressing belief in God.

Religionist—someone who trusts religion to do for him what only Christ can do.

Repentance—a change of mind evidenced by change of behavior.

Words to think about: "Repent therefore and be converted, that your sins may be blotted out, so that times of refreshing may come from the presence of the Lord" (Acts 3:19).

Resurrection—the act by which Christ rose bodily from death, showing the value of His sacrifice and His ability to live His life through all who trust Him.

Words to think about: "And with great power the apostles gave witness to the resurrection of the Lord Jesus. And great grace was upon them all" (Acts 4:33).

Salvation—God's loving offer to save from the past, present, and future effects of sin everyone who puts his or her faith in Christ.

Words to think about: "Nor is there salvation in any other, for there is no other name under heaven given among men by which we must be saved" (Acts 4:12).

Sin—any violation of God's moral laws; carries the penalty of eternal death.

Words to think about: "Therefore, just as through one man sin entered the world, and death through sin, and thus death spread to all men, because all sinned" (Romans 5:12).

Water Baptism—symbolic ceremony that is an outward declaration of personal belief in Christ.

Words to think about: "Then Simon himself also believed; and when he was baptized he continued with Philip" (Acts 8:13).

■ APPLYING IT

- Those "lists of what Christian living looks like" Mart De Haan referred to at the beginning of this chapter aren't all bad.

How can we keep high standards without being pharisaical? What should be the impetus for any standard of behavior?

- Look at the list of statements in the "Why Focus on Christ?" section. What are two or three items there that are especially helpful to you?
- How could the opposing viewpoints: "Religion Is Important; Religion Is Worthless" help you in explaining the gospel to an unsaved friend who is religious?

APPLYING for HEAVEN

IMAGINE THAT YOU ARE filling out an application to get into heaven. What would you list as your qualifications?

- I have always believed in God.
- I'm thought of as a religious person.
- I have tried to live a good life.
- I have been baptized.
- I go to church.
- I give money to good causes, even the church.
- I donate my time to help others.
- I haven't done anything really bad.
- I have friends who will vouch for me.

I hope by now you realize that if you were to list any of those qualifications on an application for heaven, you would be indicating that you don't yet understand the worthlessness of religion. You would be depending on things that, while positive and even religious, have no power to save you.

The only application that would be accepted by heaven would be one on which you listed your qualifications as follows:

- I can cite no merit of my own.
- I have been a sinner from birth.
- I am coming not in my name but in Christ's.
- I believe that Jesus is the Son of God and my Savior.
- I have accepted His sacrifice for my sins on the cross.
- I believe He rose from the dead to prove His power over sin and death.
- I have put my faith in Him and Him alone to forgive me of my sin.

If you were indicate those things, you would be showing that you have the confidence of the apostle Paul who, to distinguish between religion and Christ, wrote:

> *By grace you have been saved through faith, and that not of yourselves; it is the gift of God, not of works, lest anyone should boast. For we are His workmanship, created in Christ Jesus for good works [pure religion], which God prepared beforehand that we should walk in them (Ephesians 2:8-10).*

Which is it for you? Is there any truth to the idea that for you religion has been your method of trying to get close to God? As you look back on your life in relation to church and matters of faith, have you depended on any kind of activity, ritual, tradition, worship style, or church affiliation to save you? If so, you need to consider this single statement by Jesus Christ, who

91

said, "I am the way, the truth, and the life. No one comes to the Father except through Me" (John 14:6). Consider that the New Testament is clear in indicating that we cannot get to heaven nor can we have a personal relationship with God in any other way than through faith in the risen Savior, Jesus Christ. Religion or Christ? Which is it for you?

A MATTER OF FAITH

-

FOR PERSONAL REFLECTION